MW01199863

# She Spoke Like Poetry

by Gracie Packard

FREE AGENT PRESS

*She Spoke Like Poetry*

© 2015 by Gracie Packard

Published by Free Agent Press, FreeAgentPress.com
ISBN: 978-0692368046

Cover Photo by Gracie Packard

*Dedicated to everyone who has been generous enough to share pieces of their stories with me and those who impact my own story. You are the ones who inspire me to write.*

# Disclaimer

This didn't start out as poetry.

This didn't start out beautiful, because no matter which way you spin it blood isn't tragically glorious; it is simply an angry red.

There is nothing pretty in broken bottles and promises; nothing glimmers in cracked sobs and ribs.

But we poets, we spin sorrows into tales of glory because when brokenness is written in art, no one seems to take a second look.

And this is how we survive.

– g.p.

## *It Was Always You*

We were on fire, a supernova of passion whirling at a thousand miles a second.

We were so overwhelmed by our love that the only thing we seemed capable of was to wreck it.

We were the night sky, endless constellations of fairytale endings and bedtime stories.

But we were also trembling souls ripping apart from worry.

We were crumbling cities, ruins of a love so grand it couldn't be remembered.

We were a flickering fire at its last breath, a tree falling to the ground without warning of timber.

I should've known we wouldn't have lasted; we were too in love and blind to see.

But you were my everything; my two
a.m. secret and hiding place and you're
the reason I even started writing crooked
poetry.

## *You're Worth It*

I hope that you fall in love with someone who is crazy about you.

Someone who laughs at all your jokes even when you're not funny.

Who makes you pancakes when the world is still tired because you can't sleep and you're hungry and who doesn't mind sometimes burning a few because they're too busy dancing around in the kitchen with you.

I hope that when they look into your eyes they'll see more than the color but the galaxies lurking beneath the surface.

Fall in love with someone who tickles you when you feel like crying and who won't stop until those tears you shed are from laughter and not despair.

But who realizes that sometimes even laughter can't cure a heart that's broken and ripped.

That sometimes, not even they can heal your hurt.

But who still pushes you on swings like you were little kids, who holds your hand through the scary parts of the movies.

They better learn your favorite song but love the music your heartbeat makes even more.

Fall in love with someone who kisses you in the rain, never leaves your side, who has seen you at your worst and who still loves you and wouldn't want anyone else anyways.

### Did You Know I Would Break?

I deleted your messages last night,

But I could never delete the memories you implanted in my battered brain or the scars you left on my heart.

You left and you left me anything but a pretty sight.

## *I Don't Need Your Saving*

We spend so long looking for our Supermans, our angels in the sky that are going to swoop in and save the day.

We let them consume our thoughts and our minds and we fall and fall and we break while we wait.

We spend our entire lives hoping they'll show up, that they'll pick up our scattered pieces and glue us back together.

But there's no angel waiting in the heavens. There's no one lurking in the corner for the right moment to hug you and heal your hurt.

No one is going to run their calloused fingertips over the smooth scars and jagged cuts that line your hips like battle wounds.

You've got to be your own hero.

## *How to Break a Heart in Five Easy Steps*

1. Start by tearing down their walls. Strip
them bare, remove every inch of cracked
and dried paint, tear down the wallpaper,
smash the doors. Open them up, let them
feel safe. Ask about their quiet secrets and
memorize their favorite songs. Undo all
the coverings and bring them into the
open. Make them feel secure when they're
not hiding, when they're not camouflaged
in masks and forced smiles.

2. Tell them you love them. You've
gained their trust, you know every dusty
cobweb clad corner of their heart, you
know them better than they know
themselves. So bring out those big three
words, spell it out, muster up every
ounce of passion that's dormant in your
bones and tell them that they mean the

world to you. That your heart wants no other than them.

3. Let them get comfortable. Allow them to expect the good morning texts and the goofy pictures, make sure they become more used to your hand in theirs than walking alone. They can't feel safe by themselves anymore, don't let them keep any bit of their guard up. Don't let them rebuild that picket white fence around their heart. Don't let them think for one minute that you'll leave them.

4. Leave. Pack up. Move out of their lives, move out of the early morning kisses and the late night conversations. Don't leave behind one piece of hair, don't leave behind any explanation of your betrayal, gather up all of your gentle words and soothing touches. Don't leave behind

your love. Just leave behind a sobbing mess, leave behind a sunset awash in red blood, just leave behind a disaster.

5. Never look back.

## *I Think This is Called Destiny*

The music is five notches too loud and
my heart is beating five times too fast and
my smile's too wide to be contained on
my face and our laughter's echoing
through this town and I'm surprised it
hasn't woken up the neighbors and it's
getting late but we're so in love and your
face looks even more beautiful
illuminated by three a.m. streetlights than
I thought was possible and I didn't know
my soul was going to meet yours, but
now, in the morning with too loud music
and not enough time, I can't imagine it
any other way.

## *You've Survived Worse*

It may feel like your entire life has been ripped apart, like every shred of reality that you thought was true and right has been torn beyond recognition and that your entire world has been flipped inside out and upside down.

But maybe the only thing you can do is rip apart every single piece of false truth even more on your own and rebuild your world from scratch because it may be the only thing you can do besides drown.

## *Opposites Really Do Attract*

Maybe we weren't actually ever meant to be together.

Maybe you're just the Sun, bright and glorious for family picnics and summer memories and I'm the Moon, companion to insomniacs and restless souls.

And you see, the Sun and the Moon know each other better than they know themselves, they have spent eons sharing secrets in passing and dying so the other could live.

But their time together is limited if not nonexistent and they may be in love but the Sun can never wipe the Moon's tears and the Moon will never kiss the Sun's rays and I guess I'm just realizing no amount of love can change the inevitable.

## *We'll Learn*

See, my dear, life is a funny thing. It doesn't come with an instruction book or a how-to video. It doesn't come with any guidelines or a help hotline. You are merely thrown into this mess and expected to figure your way out without error and you will want to but oh, you can't.

You can't and you won't and it may feel hopeless.

There will be nights where all you want to do is listen to depressing songs and cry yourself to sleep and it wouldn't matter if I was by your side or not. There will be nights where your demons seem bigger than anything else, nights where they'll win in the form of despair and tears.

There will be days where you don't want to see the sun shining through your window, times when the world seems permanently colored in greys and blacks. You may feel like you're drowning while everyone else is floating, like you may never make it out alive. There will be days when that's what you'll want.

But the thing is, there will be nights when your laughter seems to wake up the world, when your smile hurts your face. You will fall in love and your heart will feel so full of joy you'll wonder why you haven't tripped and fallen on your face yet.

There will be days when the air smells like summer and the night tastes like adventure. You will dance in the rain and not care that your mascara is running. One morning you will get up before the world and drive with the music blaring and see the most beautiful sunrise.

And there will be simple nights, where

you find just the right song and have just the perfect cup of tea next to your bed and you are content just being.

Once in your life you will step on the crunchiest autumn leaf you've ever seen, you will watch the best movie you could ever imagine, that cat will choose you to be with over everyone else in the room, you will make the perfect painting, and love the most beautiful, imperfect, messy people.

This isn't an instruction manual or a set of guidelines. I haven't found that how-to video yet and I don't have the number for the help hotline. But my dear, none of us do. And I can't give you the answers, but I promise you, I will take your hand, and we will figure this out together.

## *Warning Label*

Some people smoke cigarettes, ignoring the consequences no matter how many times they're told and some people knock back shots of poison in a bar like it was candy and they were three years old. Some will hunt for drugs to calm their mind and some will pick up a gun to bide their time and they'll all search and search for the answer until death is the only answer they find.

I thought I was a little different because I just fell in love with you but I guess it's not that different after all because it's looking like it's going to kill me too.

## *Repetition*

Nothing lasts forever.

The sun sets on its day of work and the moon appears and disappears again and even this constant cycle will one day cease.

The ocean crashes onto the beach and sweeps away old shells of lives and memories.

The tears dry, the rain stops pounding, and light shines through the clouds.

Lovers come and go, leaving a mass of destruction in their careless wake, but the chaos left behind will one day end and the pieces will be put back together.

Smiles fade from a shining face and the frown that selfishly entered as the replacement falls from its spotlight of despair as well.

Good days and bad days will fill our lives without a shadow of a doubt.

But even our worst days only have 24 hours.

## *Bleeding Heart Means a Bleeding Pen*

She drowns herself in poetry and writes words onto her soul because without a pen in her hand, sorrow begins to take its toll and she's become a little too good at making broken look whole.

## *Who Exactly Decided Addiction Was Poetry?*

When you text me in the early hours of the morning and you're drunk out of your mind,

When you're struggling to form coherent sentences and your sounds slur together in a great big mess,

It's not poetic anymore.

I'm not high off of your stupid decisions and your lips don't taste any better coated with a thin layer of whiskey and cigarette smoke.

Your childish antics don't sweep me off my feet and your lack of knowledge of who this girl next to you even is doesn't do anything to the pattern of the constant thudding of the heart that is too heavy for my chest.

We aren't falling head over heels for each other. I am only struggling to keep you standing while you stumble and try to keep the poison drowning your unspoken misery down.

This isn't poetic, this isn't romantic, and neither of us are too okay anymore.

## *Oh No, I Think I've Fallen for You*

I saw the sun when it snuck over the snow brushed mountaintops early in the morning when the world was quiet.

I smiled when it struggled through the dark of rain clouds to bring a little bit of joy into this despair-ridden world.

I marveled when it glistened on top of the ocean, sparkling like a diamond.

I stared in awe when it shone through the first green leaves of summer and threw dancing shadows on the walls and trees, telling an elaborate story free for interpretation.

I didn't think it could get any better when it painted the sky an array of cotton candy colors and stopped my breath as it gave its life for the moon to shine.

But it never got any more beautiful than when the sun danced in his bright blue eyes as he looked at me like I was the only person in the world who mattered.

## *Please Don't Leave*

I don't need fame or to see my name in flashing lights.

In fact, there's nothing else in this life that I want to see.

Because I've caught glimpses of the world in your eyes,

And I think that's all I really need.

## I'll Get Over This, Just Give Me Some Time

Flicker world, with your oh so many endless nights; you show no mercy of dawn's first light.

Creaky bones moan with sorrow, hiding unknown frights; my soul is plagued with how to make this right.

And I promise I'll climb this mountain, overcome this pain, but I can't say I won't be scared by the height.

You can search for me while I mourn but I can't say you'll like what you find.

I'm not sure why this heartache tinted world turned its back on me, but I think it all went wrong when there was no more you and I.

### *The Ocean is a Liar*

Waves are relentless.

They pound and crash and destroy, taking and holding and stealing. They never cease, only calm on rare occasion.

And perhaps the calm is actually the worst because it comes in with a hidden stealth and throws you off balance when you least expect it.

Waves embody emotions in an almost scarily perfect way.

Never ending, never caring, never stopping to take account of the havoc they wreck.

They dig deep into the sand, into our hearts, carving out intricate twisting designs that write themselves on our bodies in the shape of bruises and pain.

Imprinting memories of heartache and

despair too late at night and tears and hopelessness so strong that they block out any sign of hope, any glance at the bottom of the ocean amidst the swirling chaos.

They disrupt every aspect of life, no regard of whether it's a good time to crash into the beach and bring away with it the sand and your sanity and the perfect sandcastle that you've spent years trying to build for yourself.

They leave you with the remains of a house that you put everything into, they leave you with a mess to clean up and an endless search for anything left of what you used to love.

With nothing left except for the remains of a masterpiece and debris that you didn't want in the first place, it forces you to pick yourself up, to try again, ignoring everything that tells you to quit.

### *I Suppose this is Goodbye?*

I find myself, stuck in a rut.

Thinking about you, when the clock reads
three a.m. and the house is still.

I find myself, inhaling your scent,

That still lingers on the pillow that sits,
lonesome, on your side of the bed.

I find myself, wishing for you.

You and your seemingly perfection that
has left for another.

I find myself, remembering us.

All of our adventures that left me
breathless as the sun peaked over the
mountains.

And I find myself realizing,

That I have come to be more in love with
the memories of you,

Than the person you've become.

## Oh My Grandmother, What a Big Heart You Have

Her fingertips are curled in my hair,

And I am lost in her eyes, full of danger and wanderlust and I should know not to get involved in souls such as she,

Because her fingertips and coat are rose red and blend all too well with aching blood and her laugh is crystal snow, showing mistakes all too clear.

She is beautiful and pure and my touch only dirties her; she will never scrub my stain clean.

I am simply razor sharp nails and a howling chest; I cannot be more than glistening teeth and hungry eyes and we cannot be in love.

## *But Everything Must End*

I loved you like the clouds love the sun. I loved you while I was fading and you were shining. I loved you through miles of deep blue sea and across continents. You never chased after me though; you never reached out your rays to draw me back to your warmth as I drifted away; not once did you kiss my tears as thunder crackled through my veins and rain fell from my eyes.

I loved you like the stars love the moon. I drew strength from your brightness and peace from your beauty. I loved you as my constellations of battle scars and freckles journeyed across the stretching night skies; not once did I stop to question my affection as my pieces fell away from you and slowly came back.

Little did I know that you loved the sun
far more than you ever did I.

I loved you with every fiber of my being,
I loved you until my arms trembled from
clinging to your life, and I loved you until
not one scrap of affection was left for
myself. I poured my very soul into you. I
emptied myself into a chase not worth
continuing. Oh, oh, I loved you, I did. But
you have ruined me; you have chewed
my heart up and spit it back out only to
grind it into the pavement with the heel
of your boot. You have wrecked my soul,
and it is time for me to start picking up
the pieces of the mess you made.

## *Please Come Home*

I almost called the police, sent out a search party, filed a missing persons report to bring you back home to me.

But that doesn't seem to work when your body is still here but your soul is nowhere to be seen.

### *Breathe*

Go out and lay beneath the stars, let the constellations that are made of the same stardust that fills your very body soothe your pain.

Listen to the rain pound the roof, then open the window and let yourself get soaked with water that has seen the fall and rise of empires and the fall and rise of young souls just like you.

Grab a pen or a marker or a crayon and let your hand move into scribbled letters that will turn into words that will then become a masterpiece that your very fingertips etched into the world. Don't stop until that crayon breaks or that pen runs out of ink, let the universe know that your voice will be heard.

Crawl into your bed and watch videos of cats and giggling babies and elaborate proposals until your cheeks hurt from smiling and your belly hurts from the laughter that spills effortlessly from your lips like honey on warm summer's day.

Take a hot shower and let the steam curl around you, cry until your tears mix with the water, until you can't tell them apart.

Stand in front of the mirror in nothing but your underwear because you can't deny the beauty of your skin that is stronger than anything known to man and realize that you're a goddess and that no one can break you down.

Plug in your headphones and let your head melt into your pillow and then turn the volume up until the world is drowned out, until you're sure your grandmother would have a fit about how you'll lose your hearing young. Then turn it up another notch.

Whip up a batch of your world famous

fudge brownies and throw flour around the kitchen so it looks like it snowed right inside your house and eat the whole batch by yourself while they're still warm.

Let yourself smile and laugh and cry and just be because you are beautiful and if Mozart were still alive his greatest composition would have been written to the sound of your laughter and to the beauty of your smiles and the simplicity of your tears.

And darling, oh darling.

Please remember that sometimes just getting yourself out of bed is enough and please remind yourself that you are doing the best you can and you are doing so well and you're going to make it through this.

## *I Was Born For This*

I'm a poet because I will not last, so I must create. I will perish and my scarred skin, my long hair, my green eyes–they will all decay and the only thing that will be left is unidentifiable bones.

My name will be said for the last time and my memory will fade just as summer fades into fall, slowly and unnoticed.

But the words that I etch into paper with a trembling pen will long outlive my body.

They will remain in the minds of those who continue after me. They will remain in scrapbooks of people they have impacted, in books left alone and dusty in attics.

See, I'm a poet because I am destined to die while words are destined to live.

## *Escape Route*

Shaky hands, slippery soul, trembling words, duck and roll.

Bloodshot eyes, cracking hope, spilled coffee, grab the rope.

Streaking tears, insults without a sound, another shot of whiskey, head on down.

Red stained tile, broken glass, unkept promises, jump the last.

A mess before you, light for none. When your house is no longer a home, just run, run, run.

## *The Generation of Today*

We're just bareback kids with trembling fingers and aching teeth from kissing strangers in foreign houses.

Our eyes water from the smoke filling our lungs, our hearts threaten to give up from the pain we're put them through.

We've ripped our skin and clawed at our bones to gain perfection until bits of our soul were stuck between our teeth.

Us kids, oh us shaking, sobbing, kids.

We've worked so hard to only waste it all trying to fix the problems in our heads.

## *You Bet I'm a Feminist*

You might as well stop telling me to zip
my lips shut, you might as well stop
whistling at me, I'm not a mutt. Don't you
dare tell me my shorts are just too short,
that in this shirt, my bra strap shows. I
mean, god forbid people think that me, a
girl of all things, wears a bra, because
obviously that's not something anyone
knows. And my school clearly has a right
to yell at me because my shirt is too tight,
when you ignore the fact that the boy
sitting next to me is wearing a tank top so
loose I can see all there is to offer higher
than his waist. Oh, my bad, my dear
apologies that my sharp tongue and
sarcasm isn't fit for a lady, I forgot that it
just wasn't your taste. I am tired of
hearing that she was abused and raped
because I mean, how would you feel if
someone just turned you on and then left

you? She was only 5 when it happened, does that mean that her flirtatious attitude and her short skirt caused her abuse too? It makes me sick that if a women was to ever run for the role of president, for leader of our country, there would be less talk of her political views and more of if she was fit to have such a big role, because what on earth will she do when she's on her period and too hormonal to function? To this day, a woman will get paid less than the males that work beside her doing the same job with the same skills and you're telling me you can't see the dysfunction?

Because I'm a firecracker. I am a hundred words a minute thinker, I am a go-getter and I will rip you to shreds. I will pull off every scrap on me and I will still not be asking for it clothed in threads. I am going to make my mark, I am going to be somebody, and I am going to be your boss. You are going to wish that I wasn't the one you catcalled, the one you hissed at for being a feminist when really I just wanted "an excuse to be a slut". That I wasn't the girl you decided to cross.

## *"Be Like the Snow, Beautiful but Cold"*

Do not let the world turn you cold.

Do not let it steal your hope.

Do not be the snow.

Don't let yourself become a thief of warmth, a bone chilling iciness that lets up for no one, a lonely marvel.

Instead, my dear, be the fire!

Be the child's laughter as the cold tickles her eyelashes, become the cup of hot cocoa and the warmth of the hearth.

Come out of your hibernation, let joy warm your bones and thaw your beaten soul; allow light in and laughter out.

In your quest to guard your heart from ache and hurt, please do not guard yourself from love.

My dear, do not be the snow.

Be beautiful, but don't you dare let
yourself be cold.

## *A Little Bit Lost*

Can you hear it when I speak that I'm still in love with you? Does it bleed through my veins and drip onto the cement when you look at me? Because the bitter aftertaste of rejection and loss still stings my lips and pain still threatens to crack my fragile baby bird bones and I've taken too many showers trying to scrub you off my skin but I think you can still see it in my eyes.

## *Don't Hide From Healing*

The thing about breaking is that broken pieces always find a way to be glued back together in a manner that makes it better than before. No engineer glues back his design before making it version 2.0.

You will become anew, you will be You Version 2.0, you will be all that you were but all that's left to become. Your body will become tired of crying over the same lost love, your tears will dry, your heart will stich itself back together. You will love again, in ways that you hadn't dreamt of before and, oh my, you're going to break and you're going to break hard but, oh my, one day you're still going to be okay.

## *This is What Drowning Feels Like*

It's 11:11 again and all I'm wishing for is your laugh because I know that the angels are probably singing their praises so much louder now that your joy is gracing their ears.

But you see the thing is they're already in paradise and I'm dying without you.

## *Here She Comes*

You're a storm, dark clouds looming in
the background. Your anger is thunder,
deafening cries for help, deafening shouts
of rage. Your eyes are murky pools of
grey, threatening to crack and strike
down in bright flashes of lightning. Your
tears wash away the calm of day in floods
of agony. You're wild and untamed, fury
and red hot rage, crippling pain and
destruction. But, baby, you make people
feel.

## *I Still Sleep With a Nightlight*

The nighttime is haunting.

She's a slippery serpent with fangs ready to attack, her eyes glow red and strike fear into heroes.

Her coat is filled with pockets of demons, aching for the opportunity to spring free and play.

She cackles at despair and welcomes horror with open arms.

With a swoop of her hand she steals the sun and runs away to her own desires.

She is sin and turmoil, for when the lights go down, anyone can become anything.

She is a companion to insomniacs, late night worriers and thinkers; she is awake when the loneliest people are caught in the sorrow hidden by a cloak of darkness.

The nighttime is haunting, but
sometimes, if you sit down for long
enough, she'll spin you a tale of her
adventures. For sometimes, the scariest
things have the most to share.

### *Fire Eyes*

She was reckless, her heart a firecracker
and her fingers a box of matches.

## *We Can at Least Have Fun*

Maybe we're never going to make it through this. Maybe we aren't going to come out on the other side a better person, looking back on all we went through and be glad there was nothing horrific we missed. Maybe all these trials won't be things we look back on and smile, our scars may not be tiger stripes and maybe all this inspiration is just hype. Sometimes, we don't always get our happy ending but, maybe, just maybe, our lives don't actually need any mending. Maybe it's enough to have the kiss of a lifetime even if your heart gets broken and leaves you at less than your prime. Perhaps it's okay to cry yourself to sleep some nights as long as in the morning you can remember that you're still all right. Sometimes, the rain can be just as beautiful as the rainbow, maybe the questions left unanswered are just as important as the things you know and you may die swimming for the shore but maybe the fact that you started saving yourself means even more. I guess it's just that I don't know if there's really a way to "get through this" and I don't know if "this" will ever be too different, that's all I'm trying to admit. But I guess maybe, I think it could just be enough to make the best of it.

## *Wishful Thinking*

Tonight, the sky's the kind of pretty that can't be explained in a picture.

Tonight, all that's on his mind is her.

Tonight, no sky will replace the beauty that they were.

Tonight, his pain is the kind of heavy that medicine never seems to be able to cure.

And tonight, he would give anything to have her back in his arms, to kiss her one more time, and that's the only thing he knows for sure.

## *I'm Sorry*

But darling, what did you expect when you decided my affection was the one you desired? You should've known the only thing I'm good at is turning love into fire.

## *Nothing or Everything*

I've done crazy things.

I've driven miles above the speed limit, with my arms high, my hair wild, and my voice loud.

I've run around in the snow,

With nothing but a t-shirt, frigid fingers and ears to claim, but with the warmth of laughter filling my soul.

I've been on adventures to unknown places,

Using but a guidebook in a foreign language and some companions I met just minutes previous as my way.

I've pushed the limits,

Denying rules and opposing authority, young and reckless with little concern for the consequences.

But I've never felt more alive,

Than when I was sitting with you, your
hand wrapped into mine, like
a caterpillar in a cocoon, doing nothing
but being.

### *Second Time's The Charm*

You're going to fall in love again and maybe this time you'll get it right. You're going to fall in love again with another girl, maybe another writer who's just not quite as passionate about her words as I am. Maybe she won't drown herself in them and instead drown herself in you.

Her hands won't shake; her words won't tremble.

You'll find yourself lost in her eyes because they won't hold the unspoken misery that you always discovered in mine and maybe this girl won't hold the weight of past mistakes on her shoulders like a cross, marching off to her crucifixion.

You'll kiss her in the ways I taught you just a little bit better; you'll hug her in the ways we learned just a little bit longer, and you'll love her like me just a lot bit more.

And one day, you won't even remember me.

You won't remember the night you told me you loved me or the sleepy four a.m. conversations. You'll start replacing my memory with new adventures and desires.

You will be in love and I will simply be a word on the tip of your tongue, not valid enough to be said, just a reminder of someone that you used to know.

## *It's Time For You to See, Open Your Eyes Baby*

You've let so many people stomp over you that I wonder if your fire has been put out for good;

if your passion has any hope of rekindling.

Your body has been trailed over by so many hands, so many fingers, that I wonder why it doesn't look like a child's painting.

You've let your heart flee to the east and to the west and it has migrated more miles than any bird while it made its way from lover to lover and I'm not sure if it really even knows where home is anymore.

You are worth so much,

you are worth so much more than

fleeting kisses and meaningless whispers,

you are worth so much more than picking up the pieces of your shattered heart all by yourself,

you are worth more than traveling desire and lacking passion.

### *Orion's Belt*

You have no need for starry-eyed lovers
that explode like bombs when you hold
the entire universe in your palms.

## *Ten Things I Know to be True*

1. They say that when you wake, 90% of the dream your mind conjured up while you were asleep is lost forever, but 10% never leaves and I can't help but wonder then why every single dream I've had about you seems more real than the flesh and bone standing in front of me.

2. I've been listening to the CD's you loaned me for the past three hours partly because it has my favorite artist and partly because I know he's yours and I would rather play your favorite songs than mine and maybe that's because I long to be connected to you in some way or maybe it's just because I would much rather you be happy than me.

3. When I get angry, I yell and scream
and curse but then I cry. I cry, I always
cry and I'll try to hide it from you, to keep
the salty wounds from showing because
I'm not very good at being mad but I wish
I was because it's easier to glow red with
rage than to admit you're hurting.


4. It's getting late and I should sleep but
the thoughts in a slumber-consumed
brain are much more honest than the ones
my awake eyes can filter through and I'm
not sure if I'm ready for the truth.


5. Do you remember the day where we
sat together on those lonely swing sets
and watched little kids run around
without a care in the world? We talked
about what the future looked like and
dug our toes into the sand and all I could
think about was that in twenty years I

wanted it to be you and me still on those swing sets and talking about how we had finally made it to the future, how we did it. I remember, but I doubt you do.

6. I've never felt safer than in your embrace and I've never felt more vulnerable than in your gaze and I still can't believe I let myself get close to you, I should've known better. I'm pretty stupid sometimes, but I suppose you already knew that.

7. My hands are shaking now because I can't seem to contain the whirlwind tornado of thoughts that's drumming away in my head and whenever I try to write it's nothing more than a beautiful confession. I can't separate myself from my words and I don't think I'll ever be able to become an author because of it.

8. The future is a messy thing. I still wish you were included in mine, but I need to let that fantasy go once and for all. Maybe it would help if my phone wasn't still loaded with your pictures and your scent didn't still linger on my sweatshirt and your name wasn't engraved in my heart.

9. I'm in love with you I'm in love with you I'm in love with you it's on repeat and I want it to stop I don't want to be in love with you. I don't want to be in love with you. I don't want my heart to flutter at the thought of you but my heart keeps beating beating beating and I just wish it would stop.

10. I thought you were my forever. Funny how things change.

## *No Wonder the Clouds Cry*

I feel like I've swallowed a cloudy sky, like I've consumed the weight of the rain they hold, like I've taken the grayness of their existence into my very veins.

The stunned lightning that now fills my soul doesn't light me up like a beautiful star but instead seems to be eating me alive with itching electricity and anger.

The thunder that beats in my head has left me scratching to free an ache deep within my thoughts, a pain that no matter how hard I try, I can't seem to destroy.

I've embodied a force of nature my frail bones were not meant to handle, for my heart is not able to contain something so strong and so unpredictable and my fingers weren't designed to stay stable when a storm is threatening to explode right beneath the surface.

I feel like I've swallowed a cloudy sky
and I'm realizing why the storms so often
surrender to the sun.

## *Beautiful Eyes, Broken Heart*

Oh, little sparrow girl with a fleeting heart, homesick for a place you've never been.

Small dreamer who smells like the last days of summer, your mind wanders to mysteries and sin.

Forest woman with windstorms in your veins and hurricanes in your fingertips, an entire storm aching to let go.

Coffee stained girl, a little over burnt and improperly ground but with energy to start a revolution, there isn't anything you don't seem to know.

Word crier, you taste like passion and spew hurt into stories.

Aching soul, you're so beautiful but oh so filled with worry.

## *I Guess I Was Raised to Fight*

I'm broken and my fingers shake no matter how much I focus, my knuckles are bruised, my heart has been cracked and carelessly stitched back together almost beyond recognition.

I've seen nightmares in broad daylight and wished for withheld love.

I cry when I'm angry and I'm a tidal wave of emotion.

I draw back when I'm hurt and you'll have to search for me on my worst nights at the bottom of the ocean but then I crash in and overflow on the beach.

I'm not good with words and I choke on honesty.

I'm scratched and beaten and messy.

I'm an artist: I see past the blurry exteriors and paint the true interiors.

I'm a sister: I listen with my heart and laugh with all I have.

I'm a learner: I ask the tough questions and look for the hidden answers.

I'm a daughter: I love messily and brokenly but I love completely.

I'm an adventurer: I live for late nights, forgotten maps and unforeseen memories.

I'm a friend: I reach for the bruised and sew brokenness back together.

I'm a poet: I make buildings out of agony and flower gardens out of weeds.


But I guess most of all, I'm a survivor.

## *The Beginning*

She wasn't beautiful.

She wasn't pretty,

Or nice or good or peaceful.

Normal was not in her vocabulary.


She was messy.

She looked like art,

She spoke like poetry,

She walked like music.


And she made you feel something.

# Acknowledgments

There are countless people who have aided me on both my personal and writing journey that have my eternal gratitude. However, if I were to list them all, this page alone would be longer than the entire book. As I don't think that would be the best tactic, I'll just name a few.

James Woosley, who helped me so incredibly much on this project. He helped me turn words on paper into an actual book and I will always be thankful for his confidence in me and support in this dream.

My family for putting up with me on my worst days, loving me unconditionally and encouraging me in all of the things I do. My brothers for being some of my best friends in the entire world, my dad for teaching me to never quit on my dreams, and my mom for being one of my heroes and inspiring my love of reading and writing from an early age.

Mrs. Reynolds, who is far more than an elementary school teacher. You taught me more than I ever could have expected inside and outside of your classroom and I would not be who I am today without your patience and guidance.

Kenzie, my best friend, partner in crime, cover model, and biggest cheerleader. I may be good with words, but I could never explain how much you mean to me. You've read everything I've written and forced me to keep going, both in my poetry journey and in my personal life. Here's to many more adventures with you by my side.

Liam, for being one of my closest friends and allies. You have been there for me more than I ever could have asked for and continually make me laugh when no one else can. Thanks for being tolerable most of the time and for buying me chocolate chip cookies whenever I get mad at you.

The dozens of people who have been reading my poems since the early stages and who first planted the idea of publishing them. These people include, along with many others, Jenny, Sadie, Meha, Rae, Karen, Laurel, and Rachael. With Seth, Alec, and Grace being among my biggest supporters and the ones who read all of it, not just the good stuff. None of this would have ever happened without your love and support.

I often tell people that I am simply a storyteller, I re-spin tales into poetry. Although I could never name them all, nor do I even know all of their names, I want to thank everyone who has been willing to share a piece of their lives with me. Whether it was someone I met briefly in the airport or some of my best friends who have blessed me with their adventures in life, these poems are all inspired by you. By showing me your story, I have been able to live, and write, so much more. You, my friends, are who this book is about.

Gracie Packard has loved writing for as long as she can remember (at least second grade). She currently resides in Colorado with her parents and siblings.

When she is not writing she enjoys being with her friends and family, taking pictures, listening to music, and spending time with her cat. *She Spoke Like Poetry* is her first book, but not her last.

Visit GraciePackard.com for more info.

Made in the USA
Middletown, DE
23 January 2015